T0041662

Hanuman

The Heroic Monkey God

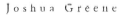

Joshua Greene

MANDALA

San Rafael

MANDALA
PUBLISHING

PO Box 3088
San Rafael, CA 94912

www.mandalaeartheditions.com

Text © Stories To Remember, Inc.
Illustrations © 2003 Indra Sharma, B.G. Sharma,
Mahaveer Swami/*Mandala Publishing*.

ISBN: 978-1-60109-030-0

Manufactured *by* Insight Editions
Printed in China

Contents

Chapter One

The Monkey Kingdom

A Devoted Warrior

Hanuman—a precocious firebrand in childhood, formidable warrior in youth, musician and scholar in adulthood, and for all eternity the embodiment of devotion—looked out at his world through eyes shining with anticipation, with a perpetual half-smile of amusement over his own prodigious abilities. One can imagine him in later years emerging from his Himalayan cave—where he is still reputed to live—scanning the horizon in search of his beloved Lord Rama, swaying gently, announcing to the world in rhythmic pulses that however well we render service there is always more to do and that life's greatest adventure is in the doing.

Hanuman happened to be a monkey—more precisely a Vanara, or member of a monkey-like tribe of forest-dwellers. Most of the time, according to reports in India's ancient texts, he was not conscious of his appearance. His simian body was important to him but incidental, like armor to a soldier or a frock to a priest. As a celibate, he held

no interest in making himself attractive to the opposite sex. And as an avid student of scripture he understood the difference between body and soul. His monkey-like nature surfaces from time to time and deserves consideration, but those who seek to know him must move past the obvious, for his story strikes at the core of human experience and at the very heart of self-discovery. ■

Traditional Story Retold

*H*anuman's story has been adapted by many traditional cultures. The oldest version is contained in the Sanskrit *Ramayana* of Sage Valmiki who lived in an ancient period of India's history. It is his 24,000-verse work that guides this retelling.

Who is Hanuman? According to Valmiki he was the child of Anjana, a celestial woman cursed to incarnate in monkey form; and Vayu, god of the wind. Setting aside theological considerations, Hanuman was the only offspring of a shunned mother and an absentee father, and he was consequently obliged to discover the world on his own. He was a mischievous child, breaking pots and helping himself to neighbors' provisions, oblivious to the havoc wrought by strength inherited from his demigod father. On one occasion he mistook the sun for a giant fruit and leaped into the sky to enjoy it. Indra, king of heaven, was flying by at that moment and, mistaking him for an adversary, knocked Hanuman back to earth. The fall broke

Hanuman's jaw (*hanu*), which earned the child his name.

Vanaras went out of their way to stay on good terms with humans and demigods such as Indra, and one can only imagine their consternation over such incidents. When the child grew fond of breaking open temple storehouses and helping himself to sacrificial offerings, Vanara priests held a meeting and agreed that something must be done. A spell was cast erasing the child's knowledge of his powers. Hanuman reached youth, then young adulthood. He studied scripture under the sun god and developed admirable skill as a musician. All this time, and despite his evident strength,

Hanuman remained unaware of his extraordinary abilities and considered himself to be nothing more than an ordinary monkey. ■

Noble Rama's Tale

The Vanaras lived in a mountain forest on the outskirts of Ayodhya, capital city of Maharaj Dasarath. This noble king, was the embodiment of dharma or righteous action, and he had four sons whom he loved dearly: Rama, his eldest; twins Lakshman and Satrugna; and Bharat, his youngest. On coming of age, Rama, the heir apparent, and Lakshman, the next in succession, entered a forest ashram for training in spiritual and martial arts. During one of their outings, Rama was introduced to princess Sita from a neighboring kingdom. The king had discovered her in a field, nestled in a furrow (*sita*). Throughout her life Sita had shown an affinity for nature. Rama found her irresistible. In a test of skill against other princes he won her hand and her heart. Rama and Sita married, to the joy of their families and subjects.

Several years passed, and on the evening before Rama's coronation, Dasarath's queen Kaikeyi reminded her husband that he had promised her two boons for once having saved his life in battle. She claimed these favors now and insisted that her son, Bharat, be crowned king instead of Rama, and that Rama be exiled to the forest for fourteen years. Dasarath staggered under the shock of this request, for Rama was his very heart. Bound by righteousness, he granted the boons and shortly thereafter died of grief. Rama worshiped his father and, entrusting the kingdom to his youngest brother Bharat, set out with Sita and Lakshman to fulfill his father's final order to leave the kingdom and live in forest exile.

Valmiki's text exalts the first years of the trio's sylvan odyssey. By some accounts the three were barely out of their teens, and they delighted in freedom from the formalities of court. During the first ten years of their journey they confronted fantastic creatures, apprenticed under mystical forest-dwellers, and grew to adulthood. Lakshman assumed the role of protector, and with no cares to trouble them Sita and Rama discovered the depth and intensity of their love for one another. Theirs was an idyllic world. With only a short time in banishment remaining, life could not have been better.

Appearances, Valmiki's story teaches, are deceiving. Their idyllic world was about to turn hideous. ∎

King of Demons

In this remote period of cosmic history miracles abounded. Monkeys talked, mountains flew, subtle pathways connected planets and a creature of chilling proportions terrorized the universe. Enter Ravana, whose very name betrayed his appetite for conquest: "He who makes the universe scream."

Ravana was born into the Rakshasa race: a subhuman species with cannibalistic instincts and deadly hungers. Ravana despised his own lower nature. Endowed with a superior intellect, he dreamed of achieving godhood. Through severe yogic practice he compelled Brahma, topmost among the demigods, to award him godlike powers and render him invincible to almost all enemy attacks The tragedy of Ravana's ambition, however, was its impossibility· biologically, psychologically, and karmically he could never be anything but a Rakshasa. So he settled for what he could achieve and surrounded himself with the trappings of his dream: wealth, power, sensual pleasures and the appearance of godhood.

Ravana built his capital on the island of Lanka, 120 miles off India's southern-most tip. His fortress, nestled on the peak of a mountain, spread out over more than 100 square miles and was protected with fortifications of gold. From Lanka he planned and launched his campaigns to conquer the universe and for generations his creature armies instilled fear and inflicted pain wherever they advanced.

When scouts reported seeing a beautiful woman and two humans in the Dandaka forest, Ravana investigated. Beautiful women bolstered his ego, and one look at Sita filled him with irrepressible desire. Sita was no mere human. She was a goddess. Having her would validate him as a god. With the help of shape-changing servants, Ravana lured Rama and Lak-

shman away from their forest dwelling, captured Sita and flew off with her to his island kingdom. Clandestinely, Sita dropped bits of cloth and jewelry as a trail for her husband and his brother to follow.

Upon returning to their cottage and discovering Sita's absence, Rama went mad with fear and reproached himself mercilessly for failing to protect her. When at last he regained his composure, he immediately set out with Lakshman to find her. Following the advice of forest guides, they approached the Vanara monkey tribe for help. ■

The Quest for Sita

At the time of Sita's kidnapping Hanuman had reached young adulthood and was serving as chief advisor to King Sugriva, leader of the Vanara community. On the day of Sita's kidnapping, Hanuman was out scouting and looked up in time to see Ravana fly over in his airship. He also observed a woman dropping bits of jewelry out of the ship. These he gathered up to show Sugriva and returned home just as Rama and Lakshma arrived. Seeing the jewels Rama clasped them, and Hanuman, to his heart. He wept and then put his story and petition before the Vanaras. Hanuman was moved by Rama's deep emotions, his eloquence and his gentle demeanor. Nonetheless, Rama was human. Could he be trusted to protect Vanara's interests, or were monkeys merely tools for helping him rescue Sita?

Sugriva made Rama an offer. A recent falling-out with his monkey brother, Vali, had him worried. If Rama agreed to kill Vali then the entire monkey army would be at

Rama's disposal. Rama agreed, and after Vali's defeat Sugriva, true to his word, organized search parties.

"You have one month," he told the scouts. "If by then you have not found Sita, return or risk my wrath."

As consolation for having lost his father, Angada, Vali's son, was invited to lead the party that would follow Ravana's southern course. Jambavan, elder king of the bear clan, would act as advisor but final decisions would be made by Hanuman.

"Be careful when you reach the southern shore," Sugriva warned Hanuman. "Those waters are infested with creatures ready to terrorize and then consume you."

Rama approached Hanuman and entrusted his royal signet ring to him as identification should he find Sita. "Take this and go with my blessings and thanks. You may be more than you know, Hanuman, and capable of doing more than you imagine." Hanuman reverentially touched the ring to his head and bowed at Rama's feet. If Hanuman had harbored misgivings about Rama, these gestures of trust went a long way toward relieving them.

During preparation for their journey, Hanuman discussed strategies for the search and rules of conduct with Rama. The young prince spoke of higher purposes, of dharma and the right of all creatures—human

از طلا گر فته باز پشتهای در همه این درهم این رفت باز نزده وام آمد

and otherwise—to live peacefully and lead a holy life. If ever a human was more virtuous, Hanuman could not say who or when. By the time his party was ready to leave, the young king had won his heart. Nothing would stand between Hanuman and his mission to find Sita.

The search party set off south over the Vindhya range of mountains, crisscrossed the desert without food or water, and had all but given up hope. The vulture Sampati told them Sita was captive on the far away island of Lanka. After many days the Vanara scouts arrived on the shore of Cape Comorin and stared out at Lanka 120 miles offshore. At seeing the vast expanse of water, their hearts sank. Could anyone make such a leap? "I could do maybe half that distance," one monkey claimed. "I could maybe go three-quarters of the way," said another. Angada, still grieving the death of his father, argued that they should give up. They could never get to Lanka. Even if they did, could anyone scout the island undetected? Was Sita even there? Their time limit had all but run out. Better to return now and avoid Sugriva's wrath. ■

Chapter Two

No Ordinary Monkey

Devoted Service to Rama

*M*eanwhile, Hanuman sat silently apart confronting his own feelings of inadequacy. Rama had awakened something in him: a love of duty, a call to service. Who was this Rama? Some said he was God himself, come to earth to restore the codes of dharma. Others called him the perfect king. Whoever he was, the more Hanuman learned of him the more attracted he was to him. A profound love had been implanted in him, a love for service to a higher cause, for "doing more than he imagined." But along with this new sensation of possibility came heavy feelings of insufficiency. Hanuman shook his head and scratched the ground. Jambavan sensed his sadness and understood.

"You can make that leap," he said, sitting down next to him, as he presented his proof. "I knew you as a child, Hanuman. You were magnificent. You were filled with strength, valor, intelligence..." Jambavan then revealed the secret of how Hanuman's powers had been suppressed, and for the first time Hanuman remembered the abilities that were his at birth. Filled with a reawakened sense of strength and purpose he swelled, grew large and bellowed out to the monkey soldiers that he would make the flight to Lanka without doubt.

Shocked from their stupor by this display, the monkeys cheered and shook their fists. Hanuman's transformation—for it was nothing less—had brought them back from the edge of oblivion. "Our mission will be achieved! Sita will be saved!" ■

The Herculean Leap

Hanuman, now in gigantic form, climbed a nearby mountain and prepared to leap. He saluted first the sun; then his father Vayu, god of wind; then Brahma, and finally all demigods and lesser beings. In true devotional form, he abandoned all pride over being the "doer" of actions and surrendered himself to becoming a transparent medium of Rama's will. He stared out, focusing on Lanka, inhaled profoundly, pressed down with his feet, shook his fur, whirled his tail. Contracting his waist, drawing in his arms and neck, and flattening his ears, Hanuman concentrated all power and energy in the lower part of his body. The mountain shook. He scanned the sky for a clear path, roared—then leaped. ■

Three Tests

If ever there were proof that Hanuman was sired by the wind, his leap to Lanka was it. Boulders shot up from the ground, propelled by the force of his spring. Animals and snakes fled in terror. His speed caused trees to lift off and swirl in the air behind him. He stretched in length, his eyes blazing like lightning, and flew.

In his journey over the ocean, Hanuman encountered and overcame three tests. The first was a mountain that rose to greet him, an offering from the ocean god as a place to rest. Hanuman politely declined, refusing to rest until his mission has been accomplished. "Rama!" he cried and flew on.

The second was Surasa, mother of serpents, sent by the demigods to test his abilities. Surasa rose up and smacked her lips. "The gods have provided me with a tasty meal," she screeched, promising to make him enter her mouth. Hanuman responded by growing larger each time that Surasa widened her jaws. When mouth and meal had reached several miles wide, he quickly shrank down to the size of a thumb, entered and quickly exited before the giant jaws could close. What tact, what courtesy! The maneuver fulfilled Surasa's promise and allowed her to depart with dignity. The serpent mother saluted him and wished him success. "Rama!" he cried again and continued on his way.

The third trial posed more lethal consequences. Simhika was an aquatic demon who fed on anything that flew over the ocean. Sugriva had warned Hanuman about this creature in preparing him for the journey south. Now, in a similar competition to see who could outgrow whom, Hanuman remembered Sugriva's warning, entered Simhika's mouth, and tore up her insides before exiting and flying on. "Rama! Rama!"

With each victory Hanuman's faith in Rama deepened, and as his faith deepened his self-confidence grew. ■

Entering Lanka

*A*s he approached Lanka, Hanuman reflected on how to best achieve his mission. Which way should he enter the city? How should he behave if captured? When should he make himself known to Sita—if indeed she were there? Despite his new-found confidence, Hanuman retained a healthy degree of caution. If it was worth doing for Rama, his instincts told him, it was worth doing right.

Hanuman landed on the island of Lanka. To pass unseen, he shrank to the size of a cat and silently entered the city. He marveled at Lanka's broad streets and towering architecture. Marble palaces supported by gold and silver columns alternated with flowering gardens and lotus-filled lakes. Hanuman entered one palace after another, astonished by floors inlaid with crystal and gems.

He entered the largest palace of all—and there lay Ravana, sleeping. It could not, Hanuman reckoned, be anyone but Ravana. Even in repose the Rakshasa king inspired awe. He was breathtaking. His imposing body was decorated with jeweled ornaments and sandalwood paste. Clothes loosely draped his prodigious form, which was surrounded by dozens of women in various stages of undress. Seeing one woman more lovely than all the others, Hanuman rejoiced, believing he had found Sita—then quickly he regained his composure, reasoning that without Rama, Sita would not eat or sleep, let alone be touched by another male.

Now Hanuman reproached himself on another level, for it occurred to him that by looking at naked women he had broken the code of dharma. He mentally reviewed his motives and decided they were pure: he was here on a mission and naked women did not distract him from his purpose. The flight to Lanka had clearly transformed him. Throughout his mission Hanuman would demonstrate similar determination, careful planning and responsible decision-making. He looked once more around Ravana's bedroom, offered prayers to Rama, and again took up the search. ■

In the Garden of Evil

Ravana's palace featured a garden of exceptional color and beauty, landscaped with flowering bushes, fruit-bearing trees and a profusion of vines. Climbing one of its trees, Hanuman heard a sigh and looking down saw a woman dressed in soiled clothes. She seemed weak, thin, and sorrowful, with eyes filled with tears. Through her

pitiful state Hanuman thought he saw something more, a profound beauty hidden beneath the squalor. Her face, though pallid, was clear like the moon. Her eyes, though heavy with fatigue, were lotus-shaped, her lips red, her waist slender. Then it struck him that this was the same woman whom he had seen on Ravana's airship.

"Sita!" he said silently.

Just as Hanuman prepared to reveal himself, Ravana entered the garden, approached Sita, and began pressing her to be his wife. Hanuman appreciated the force with which Sita rejected him, and he blanched when Ravana responded by threatening to kill her.

"You have one month to submit to

me," Ravana screamed, "or I will eat you for breakfast!"

When Ravana finally left, Hanuman considered how to best make his presence known. He must not frighten her, and he needed to overcome her predictable suspicion of his true identity as messenger of Rama. Softly, Hanuman began singing Rama's praises, telling his story beginning with their exile and ending with his own leap to Lanka. Then he jumped down, introduced himself, and presented Rama's message. "His only concern has been for your well-being," he told her. "Rama thinks of you always and bade me tell you that soon you will be together again." ■

Chapter Three

Victory For Rama

Hanuman's Gift

*S*ita interrogated Hanuman, questioning how an alliance had been made between Rama and a monkey tribe. She required Hanuman to describe Rama's distinguishing traits. Hanuman's devotion to Rama poured forth. The accord had come about, he said, thanks to Rama's profound knowledge of statecraft, military skills and scripture. His distinguishing marks were those of the ideal king: integrity and concern for all beings. As a final proof of his identity, Hanuman produced Rama's ring. Sita held the ring with tears in her eyes and, at last reassured, she smiled.

In his enthusiasm, Hanuman kneeled and offered to fly Sita away on his back. It was an innocent offer but one which distressed her, and he listened anxiously to her protestations· she doubted his ability to make the journey with additional weight, she was fearful of the flight.... Gradually Hanuman saw through these pretexts to the heart of her refusal. Sita would not let herself be touched by anyone other than Rama.

Hanuman prepared to depart then stopped, wondering if there was something more he could accomplish. By confronting Ravana could he convince the Rakshasa king to surrender Sita and thereby avoid war? It was worth a try. He drew attention by bellowing loudly, stormed through the Ashok garden, uprooted trees and tore down arches. Rakshasa guards attacked him. Hanuman allowed himself to be bound and brought before the Rakshasa king. ■

Interview with Ravana

"*What magnificence!*" *Hanuman thought* on seeing Ravana face-to-face, "What nobility, what luster. If not for his selfish ambitions, this lord of ogres could rule heaven."

"Who are you?" Ravana's minister asked. "Where do you come from? Why are you here?"

"I am the envoy of Rama, and you

would do well to heed my message."
With reason, logic and scriptural
reference, Hanuman argued that Sita
should be set free. Tactfully, he did
not accuse Ravana of abduction but
referred only to Sita's "disappear-
ance." With the skill of a seasoned
diplomat he praised Ravana's knowledge of dharma and rightful action,
urging the minister to set matters
right. When these arguments failed,
Hanuman grew more forceful and
spoke directly to Ravana.

"Your endowments do not protect you from men or monkeys," he
warned.

This reference to Ravana's per-
sonal history—and the shortcomings

of his attempts at immortality—struck a blow at Ravana's immense pride and the demon king ordered that Hanuman be put to death. Vibhishan, Ravana's pious brother, stepped forward.

"A messenger," he admonished, "is never to be slain."

Even dictators can occasionally be swayed, and Ravana reduced Hanuman's sentence from death to humiliation. "Set his tail on fire," he ordered.

When Rakshasi guards ran to taunt Sita with the news, she offered prayers to Agni, god of fire, for Hanuman's protection. Agni heard her prayers, and the flames on Hanuman's tail cooled. Hanuman broke away from his guards, resumed his gigantic form, and jumped from palace to palace setting Lanka ablaze. Only the Ashok garden was spared, for Sita's sake. Then, with a mighty leap, Hanuman flew back across the ocean like an arrow released from its bow. ■

Report to Rama

Glimpsing shore in the distance Hanuman roared, and the sound sent his monkey troops into whoops of joyful madness. Touching down, he recounted his exploits and the scouting party rushed back to Kishkinda to report the news that Sita had been found.

Hanuman bowed to Rama and

immediately reassured him of Sita's well-being, of her faithfulness and love, and then he urged Rama to act quickly to bring down the demon king and rescue her. Rama was thrilled by his report and extolled Hanuman's glories to the assembly. He declared himself incapable of repaying such service and, moved by love, embraced Hanuman deeply.

War was now unavoidable. Rama, Lakshman, Hanuman, Sugriva and his Vanara forces began preparations for one of history's most renowned military confrontations.

But how would they transport an entire army more than one hundred miles across a roiling sea? "The name of Rama can move mountains," Hanuman declared, and he began carving Rama's name on rocks and boulders. Monkey soldiers tossed them into the water, forming a solid bridge that spanned an ocean. ■

The Battle for Lanka

The ensuing battle between Rama and Ravana—a cosmic confrontation that took place on many planets and across multiple planes of reality—evolved over time into the ultimate image of good's struggle against evil. Hanuman proved himself to be a courageous and skillful warrior who, faithful to Rama's codes, never lost sight of the

protocols of combat. His most famous exploit during this epic war occurred as Rama and his forces lay dead on the plains surrounding Lanka. With his dying breath, Jambavan pointed north toward a mountain in the Himalayas.

"All may yet be saved," the old bear king said, "if you bring a life-giving herb that grows only on that peak."

Hanuman arrived on the mountain but was unable to identify the herb. True to form and always loving a challenge, he uprooted the entire mountain and carried it back to Lanka. Speed of flight heated the herb, and its aroma revived Rama and the entire monkey army. The battle's climax pitted Rama in hand-to-hand combat against Ravana and ended with Ravana's death by Rama's arrows.

Sita escaped from the Ashok garden and was reunited with her beloved Rama. Pious Vibhishan was installed as Lanka's new king, and after their return to Ayodhya, Hanuman was guest of honor at Rama and Sita's joyous coronation. ■

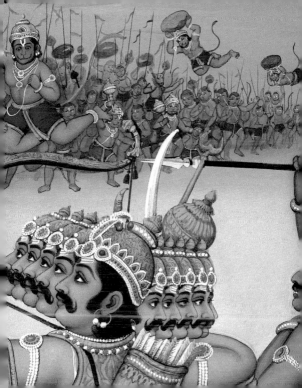

Mission Fulfilled

Rama and Sita ruled for many years.
Sita bore twin sons. The citizens of
Ayodhya regained their happy, peace-
ful lives. Hanuman returned to Kishkinda, and may, from time to time,
have visited Ayodhya where he would
have received a hero's welcome.

That is one ending to Valmiki's
story.

In another, a final chapter so tragic that some scholars doubt its provenance, citizens of Ayodhya began questioning Sita's chastity. Had she not been Ravana's privileged prisoner? Who knew what transpired during those months together? To quell their discontent, Rama banished Sita, now pregnant with their twin sons, to the forest. Eventually their separation was more than Rama could bear. He proposed that if she survived a test of fire and thus demonstrated her purity, Sita could rejoin him on the throne. When Rama's messenger arrived at her forest home, Sita took no pleasure in hearing his offer. Throughout their life, through epic trials and tragedies, Sita had proven herself Rama's equal in every way. Was this how he honored their partnership, with banishment and tests of fire?

At the appointed time, she stood before Rama and the citizens of Ayodhya. "If I am guiltless," she announced, "then let Mother Earth from whom I sprang receive me back." The ground opened. Bhumi, goddess of the earth, emerged, embraced her daughter, and together they descended into the elemental kingdom that was their home.

Rama never recovered from Sita's departure. In due course he and his brothers turned control of the kingdom over to their sons, and Rama prepared to die. Learning of his decision,

Hanuman, Sugriva and the Vanara monkeys rushed to Ayodhya.

"Live," Rama told a teary-eyed Hanuman. "Stay here and rejoice as long as my story is told." With that, he entered the gentle waters of the Sarayu River which flowed nearby. And all the Vanaras and all the citizens of Ayodhya followed him. ■

Another Mission Begun

*O*vertly, Hanuman's mission on behalf of Rama was accomplished when the battle for Lanka was won. On a deeper level, another mission had just begun. With time, Hanuman's exploits followed a classic evolution from experience to memory, from memory to art, and from art to myth. New episodes in his saga were added along the way, new versions of his story emerged in retellings around the Indian subcontinent. Hanuman's glories migrated to Thailand where the local version of *Ramayana* is called *Ramakien*; to China where he is known as Shun-woo Kong, the Wind Monkey. Buddhism's *Sunya Purana* portrays him as a gatekeeper and as Buddha's minister. His evolution to demigod status prompted construction of temples in his honor and hymns in his praise. As his identity and purpose evolved within various communities, Hanuman worship developed into a religion of its own.

Depending on whose calculation one chooses to believe, Hanuman's story took place some time between

7,000 BC and 1,000,000 BC. He has been sighted on occasion since then. In *Mahabharata*, a story which took place several thousand years after the battle for Lanka, an elder Hanuman is described living in the Himalayas, somewhat grayer but strong as ever. Today he is known as "the remover of obstacles." His reputation for aggressive action has earned him an iconic role among wrestlers and political militants. Students pray to him for good grades in school. Comic strips depict him as a simian superhero. More than a messenger of Rama or servant of monkey king Sugriva, he is now *Bhakta Avatar*, the personification of devotion. Perhaps Hollywood icons such as King

Kong, Mighty Joe Young, and more recently Chewbacca of *Star Wars* fame owe their origin to this remarkable monkey hero from remote history.

Is he there now? Does he stand outside a cave in the Himalayas and scan the horizon in search of his beloved Lord Rama? Does he cry out, "I stay in this world, Rama, just to tell your story!"

What is certain is that he dwells forever in the hearts of those who, like him, desire freedom from diabolical Ravanas, strive to serve Rama and the cause of righteous action, "do more than they imagine," and who are always ready to embark on life's great adventure. ■